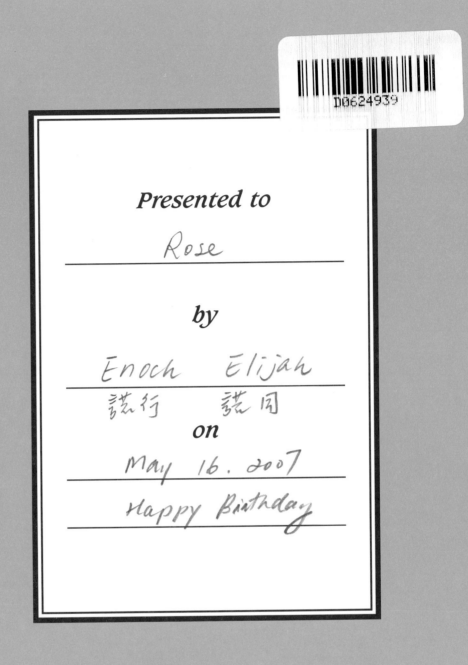

Presented to

Rose

by

Enoch   Elijah

諾行   諾同

on

May 16. 2007

Happy Birthday

D0624939

The Bible & Me
Picture Book

Stories by *Wanda Hayes*
Illustrated by *Frances Hook*

STANDARD PUBLISHING
Cincinnati, Ohio

Illustrations by Frances Hook
Design by Coleen Davis and Dale Meyers

The Standard Publishing Company, Cincinnati, Ohio
A division of Standex International Corporation

© 1998 by The Standard Publishing Company
All rights reserved
Printed in the United States of America

05 04 03 02 01 00 99 98   5 4 3 2 1

Library of Congress Cataloging-in-Publication Data
Hayes, Wanda.
    The Bible and Me picture book / stories by Wanda Hayes ;
[illustrations by Frances Hook].
        p.   cm.
    Summary: Presents Bible stories from the Old and New Testaments,
stories with lessons about modern-day children, and prayers.
    ISBN 0-7847-0799-5
    1. Bible stories, English.   2. Children--Prayer-books and
devotions--English.   [1. Prayer books and devotions. 2. Bible
stories.] I. Hook, Frances, ill.   II. Title.
BS551.2.H393   1998
242' .62--dc21   98-13272
                                                    CIP
                                                    AC

Materials may not be reproduced in whole
or in part in any form or format without
special permission from the publisher.

Bible Stories

Thank You Stories

Bible Stories

Noah Built a Boat

Many, many years ago God spoke to a good man named Noah. He said, "Noah, I want you and your three sons to build a big boat. This boat will be a house for you, your wife, and your sons and their wives."

Noah and his sons obeyed God. They built a big boat just as God told them. When it was finished, God said, "Take two of every kind of animal and bird into the boat; take enough food for your family and for the animals." Noah did just what God said.

When Noah and his family and all the animals were inside the big boat, God closed the door. Soon Noah and his family heard, "Pitter patter, pitter patter." It was the sound of rain, and it grew louder and louder. It rained and it rained. It rained for forty days and forty nights. But Noah and his family and all the animals in the big boat were safe and dry.

After the rain stopped, the big boat came to rest on top of a mountain. When the land was dry again, Noah and his family came out of the boat. All of the animals and birds came outside too. Noah prayed, "Thank you, God, for taking care of us."

From Genesis 6:13–8:22

MCMLXIII, The Standard Publishing Company

Jacob and Esau

Isaac and Rebekah were very happy. God gave them two strong baby boys. They were twins. One was named Esau and the other one was named Jacob.

God told Rebekah, "Your sons will be the leaders of two big groups of people someday."

Rebekah took good care of the sons God had given to her and Isaac. She taught them to love and obey God.

Jacob was a very quiet boy, who liked to stay near his tent and take care of sheep.

Esau liked to go into the fields and hunt animals for food, as his father did.

Rebekah watched Jacob and Esau grow. She was very pleased with her two sons. Isaac was very pleased with his two sons.

And when Jacob and Esau grew up and became men each of them was the leader of a big group of people, just as God had promised.

From Genesis 25:19-27

© MCMLXIII, The Standard Publishing Company

Baby Moses

Long ago a kind mother carried a little basket bed she had made for her baby boy. The mother and her daughter walked to the river with the baby in the basket bed.

"Shhh! Don't cry," the mother said to the sweet baby. "Go to sleep. God will take care of you." Then she set the basket bed on the water, among the tall grass. She was hiding her sweet little boy so the wicked king would not kill him. "Miriam, stay close and watch your baby brother," the mother said.

The baby's mother left, and Miriam watched the little basket bed very closely. Soon a princess came to the river. "What do I hear?" she said. "It sounds like a baby crying." The princess looked and saw the basket bed. She saw the sweet little baby boy. "I will not let the king hurt you," the princess said.

Miriam said, "I know a good nurse who will take care of the baby for you."

"Go and bring her," said the princess.

Do you know whom Miriam brought to take care of her brother? Her very own mother! She must have thanked God very much for letting the princess find the baby.

The princess said, "I shall name the baby Moses."

And Moses grew to be a good helper for God.

From Exodus 2:1-10

© MCMLXIII, The Standard Publishing Company

Ruth Helped Naomi

"Good-by," said Naomi. "I must go back to the city where I used to live. You must go to your city, too, Ruth."

"No," said Ruth. "You are my dear friend, and I shall not leave you alone. I will go home with you. Your friends will be my friends. I will love and obey God as you do."

So Naomi and Ruth, two women who loved God, walked together to Bethlehem where Naomi used to live.

"Look, it is our old friend, Naomi," the women in Bethlehem said.

And Naomi said, "This is my friend, Ruth. She has come to live with me so I will not be lonely."

Ruth did something else for Naomi, too. When they needed food, Ruth went to a field where the men gathered tall, yellow grain. Sometimes they left a little grain on the ground. Ruth was allowed to have it. She gathered the grain in her apron and took it home to Naomi. Naomi made flour from the grain, and she made bread from the flour.

Ruth and Naomi said, "Thank you God, for taking care of us." And Naomi prayed, "Thank you God, for my dear friend, Ruth."

From Ruth 1, 2

MCMLXIII The Standard Publishing Company

Hannah's Prayer

Hannah wanted a baby boy more than anything else in the world. So when Hannah and her husband went to God's house to worship, Hannah kneeled and prayed to God. She said, "God in heaven, please give me a baby boy. I shall take care of him and teach him to love you. He will work for you all his life."

Hannah and her husband went home. One day God gave Hannah a little baby boy, just as she had wanted. Hannah was very happy. She said, "I shall call the baby Samuel."

Hannah took good care of Samuel. She fed him and washed him and put clean clothes on him.

When Samuel was a little boy, his mother dressed him in his best clothes and took him to God's house. Hannah went to keep her promise to God. She said to Eli, the man who took care of God's house, "This is the boy God gave me. This is the boy I prayed for. Take care of him and teach him how to please God."

And Eli did take care of Samuel. Samuel lived in God's house and became a good helper for God.

From 1 Samuel 1

© MCMLXIII, The Standard Publishing Company

Samuel Heard God Call

Samuel liked living in God's house. He liked helping Eli. There was a lot of work to do, and Samuel was a good worker.

Samuel opened the big doors of God's house in the morning. Perhaps he helped sweep the floors and dust the furniture. Samuel did whatever Eli told him to do. There were many ways a boy like Samuel could help.

One night after Samuel had gone to bed, he heard a voice call, "Samuel."

Who could it be? Samuel sat up in bed. "It must be Eli," he thought. So Samuel called out, "Here I am." And he ran to Eli's bed and said, "I came because I heard you call me."

But Eli said, "I did not call you, Samuel. Go back to bed."

Again the voice called, "Samuel."

Samuel hurried to Eli, but Eli said, "I did not call you, my son. Go back to bed."

The voice called Samuel again. But this time Eli told Samuel, "Go back to bed, and when you hear the voice again, say, 'Speak, Lord, for your servant hears you.'"

And that's what Samuel did. It was God's voice calling him. God had a special message to tell His good helper, Samuel.

From 1 Samuel 3:1-10

MCMLXIII, The Standard Publishing Company

David Sang About God

David was a shepherd boy. He took care of his father's sheep. He led the sheep and the little lambs to green fields where they ate all the green grass they wanted. And when the sheep were thirsty, David took them to a stream of water to get a drink.

Sometimes David made songs and sang them to his sheep while he played his harp. David sang many songs about God. When David thought about God, he felt just like a sheep; and God was the shepherd who took care of him. David wrote this song about God:

God is my shepherd; I do not need anything.
He leads me in green fields and by still waters.
He makes me strong.
He teaches me to do what is right.
I shall never be afraid of bad things because God is with me.
I am very happy.
God will be good and kind to me all my life,
And I shall live in the house of God forever.

From Psalm 23

CMLXIII, The Standard Publishing Company

David Became a King

David took care of his father's sheep near the town of Bethlehem. David obeyed his father, and he obeyed his heavenly Father, God.

Because David was good, God took care of him. When a lion took one of David's sheep, David went after the lion and killed it. He brought the sheep safely back home to the other sheep. God helped David kill the lion. When a bear took one of David's sheep, God helped David kill the bear.

One time while David was watching his sheep, someone came running toward him calling, "David, David, come to your house. A man has come to visit your father, and he wants to see you."

When David came to the house, he met the man. He was Samuel, who had been a boy in God's house. Now Samuel was an old man. God had sent Samuel to find the next king for His people. And David, the shepherd boy, was the one God had chosen.

"When you are a man, you will be the king," Samuel told David.

God was pleased with David. David was a good shepherd boy, and God knew he would be a good king.

From 1 Samuel 16:1-13; 17:34-37

MCMLXIII, The Standard Publishing Company

Elisha Healed Naaman

Naaman was the captain of an army of the king. He was a great man, but Naaman was very sick. A young girl who helped take care of Naaman's wife said, "I wish that Naaman could visit God's helper, Elisha, in my country. He would make Naaman well."

When Naaman heard what the little girl said, he decided to go see Elisha and find out whether he could make him well. So Naaman rode to the land where Elisha lived.

When Elisha heard that Naaman was in his country, he sent someone to tell Naaman, "Go and wash seven times in the Jordan River, and you will be well."

But when Naaman heard this, he was angry. "I thought Elisha would come and make me well. I do not want to wash in the Jordan River."

Naaman's servant said, "Elisha did not tell you to do something hard. Do what he said."

So Naaman obeyed Elisha. He went to the Jordan River and washed—one time—two times—three times—four times—five times—six times—seven times.

When Naaman came out of the water the seventh time, he was well. Naaman could hardly believe it.

He was so happy he went back to Elisha and said, "I know that there is one God. God made me well."

Naaman was glad God made him well, and he was thankful for the little girl who helped him.

From 2 Kings 5:1-15

MCMLXIII, The Standard Publishing Company

Elisha's Kind Friends

Elisha walked through many towns telling people how to obey God. Everyone who saw Elisha knew that he was a good man.

One day when Elisha came by a house, the woman who lived there said, "Hello, Elisha. Come and eat with my husband and me. We are glad to share our food with you. Come and rest in our house. You must be tired.

So Elisha ate with the man and woman. And every time Elisha walked through that town, he ate with them.

One day the woman said to her husband, "Elisha is one of God's helpers. Let's help him by building a little room for him. We can put a bed, a table, a chair, and a lamp in the room. Then Elisha will have a nice place to stay when he comes here again."

The next time Elisha visited the man and woman, they said, "Elisha, we have a surprise for you. We have built your own room with a bed, a table, a chair, and a lamp. We want you to use this room because you are God's helper."

And every time Elisha visited the man and woman, he stayed in his own nice room. And Elisha prayed, "Thank you, God, for these kind people and for this room."

From 2 Kings 4:8-11

CMLXIII, The Standard Publishing Company

Daniel Prayed to God

Daniel prayed to God every morning, every afternoon, and every night. Daniel thanked God for many things.

In the country where Daniel lived only a few people prayed to God. Some people did not like Daniel. They asked the king to make a law saying that anyone who prayed to God would be put into a den of lions.

But Daniel was not afraid. Every day he prayed three times in front of the window. He thanked God just as he always did.

Then the king had to put Daniel in the den of lions. But the king was a friend of Daniel. He did not want Daniel to be hurt. The king was sorry he had made the law. He was sorry that his friend Daniel was in the den of lions.

After Daniel had been in the den of lions all night, the king hurried there and called, "Daniel, did your God take care of you?"

"Yes" said Daniel. "God sent an angel to shut the lions' mouths. They did not hurt me."

Then the king let Daniel go back to his house. And every day Daniel knelt in front of the window and prayed three times to God, just as he always did.

From Daniel 6

MLXIII, The Standard Publishing Company

The Mother of Jesus

Long ago there was a young woman named Mary. She was a very good woman.

One day God sent an angel to Mary. She must have been surprised to have an angel visit her, for the angel said to her, "Do not be afraid, Mary."

Then the angel told Mary, "God is very pleased with you. He has chosen you to be the mother of a very special baby boy. His name will be Jesus. He will be God's own Son."

After the angel spoke, Mary was so happy that she wanted to sing. "I will be very glad to be the mother of Jesus," she said.

Mary knew God would help her to be a good mother. She may have prayed, "Thank you, God, for this good news."

From Luke 1:26-38

MLXII, The Standard Publishing Company

Baby Jesus

Mary and her husband, Joseph, came to the city of Bethlehem. There were so many people in Bethlehem that Mary and Joseph had to sleep in a stable. Cows and sheep lived in the stable. But there was room for Mary and Joseph. And there was soft, warm hay to lie down on.

"Ummm, the hay smells sweet," said Mary.

"I am glad to have a nice place to rest," said Joseph.

That night in the warm stable in Bethlehem, a baby boy was born to Mary. He was the special baby boy God had promised. Mary wrapped Him in soft cloth and laid Him in a manger filled with soft, warm hay.

"Hello, baby Jesus," said Mary and Joseph.

"Baa, baa," said the sheep softly.

Baby Jesus was asleep.

From Luke 2:1-7

MLXII, The Standard Publishing Company

Happy Shepherds

On a grassy hillside some shepherds were taking care of sheep. They did not want the sheep to get lost. They did not want a wolf to hurt the sheep.

Suddenly there was a shining angel standing by the shepherds. They were afraid.

"Don't be afraid," said the angel. "I have good news to make everybody in the world happy. Tonight in Bethlehem Jesus has been born. You will find Him wrapped in soft clothes and lying in a manger."

And suddenly there were many, many angels. They said a special thank you to God because Jesus was born.

When the angels were gone, the men who took care of the sheep weren't afraid any more. "Let's go see the baby the angel told us about." And they hurried as fast as they could.

After the shepherds saw the baby Jesus sleeping in the manger, they said a special thank-you to God. They were very happy.

Luke 2:8-20

MCMLXII, The Standard Publishing Company

A Visit to the Temple

Mary picked up Jesus from the bed where He had been sleeping. She wrapped Him in new, clean clothes. Today was a special day for the baby Jesus. Today Joseph and Mary would take Him for a visit. They would take Him to the temple.

The temple was shiny and clean. In one part some people were praying. In another part some people were singing to God.

Mary and Joseph made a promise at the temple. "We will take good care of Jesus. We will teach Him to love and obey God."

God heard Mary and Joseph's promise. God knew Mary and Joseph would take good care of His Son, Jesus.

From Luke 2:22

© MCMLXII, The Standard Publishing Company

A Happy Mother

Mary held little baby Jesus in her arms. She thanked God many times for choosing her to be Jesus' mother.

Mary felt very happy to be the mother of God's own Son. She took very good care of baby Jesus. She fed Him. She rocked Him in her arms so He could go to sleep. She may have sung songs to Him to make Him happy.

Mary watched everything that Jesus did. Jesus grew just as you did when you were a baby. Sometimes He laughed and sometimes He cried. Sometimes He kicked His feet.

Mary may have held Jesus close to her every day and said, "I love you, baby Jesus."

Baby Jesus felt very happy in His mother's arms.

From Luke 2:40

© MCMLXII, The Standard Publishing Company

A Good Son

The first time Jesus went to the temple, He was a little baby. After that visit, Jesus and Mary and Joseph lived in Nazareth. And God blessed Jesus. He grew and be came strong. And He was very wise.

At last Jesus was twelve years old. "Today is the day, Jesus," said His mother. "Today you may go with Joseph and me to worship in the temple."

Jesus was glad that He could go to the temple and pray to God just as Mary and Joseph had done when He was a little baby.

It took many days to go to Jerusalem. Jesus was very glad to be there. Most of all He was glad to be in the temple worshiping God. Jesus prayed to God, for He liked to talk to His Father in heaven.

Jesus obeyed God. He obeyed Mary and Joseph. Jesus was a good son. Mary and Joseph were pleased with Him. And God was pleased with His Son.

Luke 2:41-52

© MCMLXII, The Standard Publishing Company

The Woman by a Well

After Jesus grew to be a man, He traveled all around the country teaching the people about His Father, God. Jesus' friends went with Him. They walked along the hot, dusty roads.

One day when Jesus and His friends had walked for a long time, they stopped at a well to rest.

A Samaritan woman came to fill her pitcher. Jesus was thirsty. He said to the woman, "Give me a drink."

The woman was surprised. "Why do you speak to me—someone you don't even know?" she asked.

"If you knew who I am, you would have asked me for something," Jesus said, "something much better than a drink of water."

Jesus and the woman talked for a long time. And Jesus told the woman many things about herself. All the time Jesus was talking, the woman may have been thinking "I know He is someone great." Then the woman said to Jesus, "I know that God promised to send Jesus, who will tell us everything."

Jesus must have looked at the woman very kindly as He said, "I am Jesus."

The woman had found something much better than water. She found Jesus, God's own Son.

From John 4:5-26

© MCMLXII, The Standard Publishing Company

Jesus Made a Boy Well

One day a rich man, who worked for a king, came to Jesus and said, "My son is sick in another city. Please come and make him well. He is so sick that his mother and I are afraid he will die."

Jesus knew that the rich man believed He could make his son well. So Jesus told the man, "Go home. Your son is alive."

The rich man believed Jesus. He hurried back to his own city as fast as he could. And before he even got to his house, his servants came and said, "Your son is alive. He is all right."

The rich man knew Jesus had made his son well. And everyone in his house knew that Jesus had made the little boy well.

Now the little boy could run and play again. He could hug his father and mother. He could do everything he used to do. The rich man and his wife and little boy were very happy. They were very thankful for Jesus.

From John 4:46-54

© MCMLXIII, The Standard Publishing Company

One Boy's Lunch

Wherever Jesus went crowds of people followed Him. Some came to hear Him tell about God and about how they should live. Sick people came to Jesus so He would make them well.

One day a big crowd of people listened to Jesus nearly all day. Jesus taught the people, and He healed some of them. The people were so interested in Jesus they didn't even go home to eat. Jesus knew the people were hungry so He asked His helpers, "Where can we buy bread for these people?"

Philip said, "We do not have enough money to buy even one bite of bread for everyone."

Then Andrew said, "There is a boy here who has five loaves of bread and two fish. But they will not feed all of these people."

Jesus took the bread and fish the boy gave to Him. Then He told everyone to sit down on the soft grass. Jesus thanked God for the boy's lunch.

Then something very special happened. Jesus gave His helpers the bread and fish to give to the people. Instead of five loaves and two fish, there were more and more. There was enough for everyone. There were even twelve baskets full of food left after everyone had eaten.

The people knew that only God could have made so much food from one boy's small lunch.

From John 6:1-13

MCMLXIII, The Standard Publishing Company

A Kind Shepherd

One time Jesus told this story: "There was a shepherd who took care of one hundred sheep. Early in the morning he led them out of their fold into the fields.

"The shepherd loved to walk with his sheep through the fields where they could eat soft, green grass. He loved to sit by a cool stream of water where the sheep could get a drink. 'Baa, baa,' said the daddy and mama sheep. 'Maa, maa,' said the baby lambs.

"When the day was almost over, the shepherd took his sheep back to the fold. As they went in the gate, he counted them, 'One, two, three, . . .' all the way up to ninety-nine. That's all there were. One sheep was gone.

"The kind shepherd went to find his lost sheep. He looked in the big grassy field. He looked by the stream. He climbed up the rocky hillside. 'I'm coming!' he called.

"Soon the shepherd found the poor, scared sheep. He lifted him very carefully to his shoulder. 'I will take you back home now.'

"'Baa, baa,' said the sheep. 'Thank you.'

"The sheep was happy, but the shepherd was the happiest of all."

From Luke 15:3-6

MCMLXII, The Standard Publishing Company

"Thank You!"

Wherever Jesus went people said, "Please make me well," and Jesus did. He made blind people see. He made lame people walk. He made dead people alive. The people knew God's Son could do these things.

One day as Jesus and His friends started to go into a city, they heard some men call, "Jesus, teacher, help us." Jesus saw ten men who were very sick. They had bad sores on their bodies.

Jesus told them, "Go, show yourselves to the priests." The men did what Jesus said, and as they started to walk away they looked at their bodies. The sores were all gone. Jesus made all ten men well. How happy they were!

Nine of the men hurried on into the city to show their friends they were well. But one man came running back to Jesus. He lay down on the ground at Jesus' feet and said, "Thank you, Jesus. Thank you for making me well."

Jesus was sorry that nine of the men didn't say "thank you." But He was very glad that one man did. Jesus knew this man really loved Him.

From Luke 17:11-19

ACMLXII, The Standard Publishing Company

A Man in a Tree

"Jesus is coming!"

"The Master is coming," all the people were saying. They were excited. Soon everybody knew that Jesus was in their city. Men and women, boys and girls crowded along the street to see Jesus.

"I want to see Jesus, too," thought Zacchaeus. "But all of these tall people are in front of me, and I am too short to see over their heads." Zacchaeus was a very short man. "I have heard so many wonderful things about Jesus," said Zacchaeus. "I must see Him."

Zacchaeus looked around. "I know how I can see Jesus." And he climbed a tall tree by the street.

Zacchaeus looked far down the street. Several men were coming. One of them was Jesus. Soon He would walk right under the tree where Zacchaeus was. But Jesus didn't walk by the tree. Instead He stopped underneath it, and He looked up at Zacchaeus. Jesus said, "Zacchaeus, hurry and come down for I'm going to stay at your house today."

Zacchaeus did hurry down from the tree, and Jesus did stay at Zacchaeus' house that day. Zacchaeus was very glad he climbed the tree to see Jesus.

From Luke 19:1-10

MLXII, The Standard Publishing Company

Jesus and the Children

"Go to Jesus," said the mothers. "Go with the other children."

Jesus was sitting on a large stone. He saw the mothers bringing their little babies to Him. He saw other boys and girls coming to Him. Jesus loved them.

But Jesus' helpers stood in front of Him and said, "Don't bring the children to Jesus today. He is tired. Let Him rest. Go back to your mothers, children. Go on now. Leave Jesus alone."

Jesus did not like what His helpers said. He said to them, "Let the children come to me. Don't stop them."

And the children ran to Jesus. He asked God to bless each one of them. Then Jesus put His hand on each little boy and each little girl. He put His arms around them. Jesus smiled at one little girl as He held her face with His hands. "I love you, Jesus," she said.

From Matthew 19:13-15 and Mark 10:13-16

© MCMLXII, The Standard Publishing Company

A Song for Jesus

It was a special day in Jerusalem. Jesus was coming to worship in the temple. When the people heard Jesus was coming, they went out to meet Him. They spread their coats down on the road. These made a special carpet for Him to ride on—just like a king. Some of the people cut branches from trees and laid them in the road for Jesus.

Then Jesus came riding on a donkey. There were many, many people. They were so glad that they shouted, "Hosanna to the son of David. Hosanna in the highest." This was how they showed Jesus they loved Him. They knew he was very great.

Jesus got off His donkey and walked into the temple. Many sick people came to Him, and He made them well. And all the time He was in the temple, Jesus heard the children singing to Him, "Hosanna to the son of David. Hosanna!" The children knew Jesus was their friend. He liked their song.

From Matthew 21:6-11, 14-16

LXII, The Standard Publishing Company

A Lesson Jesus Taught

Jesus and Peter and John and Jesus' other friends were eating together. After supper Jesus took a towel and a pitcher and poured clean water into a bowl as Jesus' friends watched.

"What is He going to do?" they may have said to each other. Soon they knew.

Jesus began to wash His helpers' feet with the water and dry them with the towel. That was a good thing for Him to do because their feet got dirty walking along the dusty roads. The cool water felt very good.

When Jesus washed Peter's feet, Peter said, "Why are you washing my feet?" Peter didn't think Jesus should do a job like that because He was God's own Son.

After Jesus washed the feet of all His friends there, He sat down again and answered Peter's question. "I have washed your feet to teach you to do kind things for each other and other people."

Jesus' friends did obey Him. They were kind to each other. They were kind to other people, too. And they always remembered the time Jesus washed their feet.

From John 13:3-17

© MCMLXII, The Standard Publishing Company

The Good News

Jesus' friends were very sad. They thought they would never see Jesus again. They thought they would never be happy again.

One morning Mary and some other friends of Jesus heard the good news. The women heard that they would see Jesus again. They ran to tell the good news to other friends of Jesus.

Suddenly the women stopped because someone was standing in front of them. It was Jesus! The women could hardly believe that Jesus was really there. But He talked to them. He said, "Tell my friends that I will meet them soon."

The women worshiped Jesus. They were happy that Jesus had come back to see them.

From Matthew 28:1-10

MCMLXII, The Standard Publishing Company

A Prayer by Jesus

Jesus was God's own Son, and He talked to God the way we do. He prayed to Him. Jesus prayed to His Father every day.

One day Jesus walked along a road with two of His friends. He talked with them about the Old Testament. The men loved to hear Jesus teach. They listened to everything He said.

When Jesus and the two men came to the city, one of the men said, "Come and eat supper with us."

Jesus probably said, "Thank you," because they invited Him to stay with them.

Before the men ate, Jesus bowed His head and thanked God for the food as He always did. Perhaps He said, "Thank you for this bread, my Father. Thank you for my kind friends."

And Jesus' friends may have said, "Thank you, heavenly Father, for Jesus."

From Luke 24:13-15, 28-30

MCMLXII, The Standard Publishing Company

Timothy

Timothy was a good boy. He had a kind mother named Eunice and a kind grandmother named Lois. Timothy's mother and grandmother loved and obeyed God. They both taught Timothy to love and obey God.

Timothy loved to hear his grandmother read from God's book. She read stories about Moses and Samuel and David and many other helpers of God. Perhaps Timothy thought, "Maybe someday I can be a helper for God. Maybe I can be as brave as the men God's Book tells about."

Timothy grew older. He learned more and more about God's Book. He learned to read and study it by himself. One day a man named Paul came to the town where Timothy and Eunice and Lois lived. He taught Timothy and his mother and grandmother about Jesus, God's Son. Paul said, "Timothy, you can tell others about Jesus, too. Come and help me teach people in other countries how to obey God."

Timothy was very excited. "Paul wants me to go with him," thought Timothy. So Timothy and Paul traveled to many different cities and countries. Sometimes they walked, and sometimes they sailed on a ship. Timothy and Paul taught many people about Jesus. Timothy was a good, brave helper for Paul and for God.

From Acts 16:1-5; 2 Timothy 1:3-5

ILXIII, The Standard Publishing Company

Dorcas Helped People

"Look at the dress Dorcas made for me!" said a happy little girl. "I love kind Dorcas. She made my pretty new dress."

Dorcas was a very good woman. She used her hands to help people in a special way. Dorcas made clothes for women who did not have much money. And she made coats and dresses for poor children, too. Dorcas had many friends because she was so kind.

But one day Dorcas' friends were very sad. Dorcas was very, very sick. Soon Dorcas died. Her friends looked at the pretty coats and dresses Dorcas had made them. The people cried. "We will miss our good friend very much," they said.

But something happened. Two men brought Peter, one of Jesus helpers, to Dorcas' house. Peter went to the room where Dorcas was in bed. He knelt down and prayed to God. Then Peter said to Dorcas, "Get up."

And she did. Dorcas was alive again! Peter took Dorcas to her friends. Oh, how happy they were! They told everyone they saw, "God made Dorcas alive again. Our friend Dorcas is alive."

From Acts 9:36-42

© MCMLXIII, The Standard Publishing Company

Do You Remember?

Try to remember the names if you can.
Then have someone read you the stories again.

Who lived in a boat with animals in it?
Who made a boy well again in a minute?

Name the twin boys who lived in a tent.
Who taught about Jesus wherever he went?

What baby slept in a basket bed?
Whom did Peter pray for when she was dead?

Who gathered grain for her friend every day?
Who kneeled by his window three times to pray?

Who prayed for a son—her only wish?
Who fed a crowd with five loaves and two fish?

What boy answered God when He called him one night?
Who made a man wash to make him all right?

What boy sang to God while he cared for his sheep?
Who gave Elisha a good place to sleep?

Every kind person in God's Book is true,
And each one of us can be God's helper, too.

Thank You Stories

God Gave Me Mommy and Daddy

Thank you, Mommy, for washing my face.
Umm! The soap smells good.
Thank you for putting my Sunday clothes on me.
I'll stand still for you.
Thank you for combing my hair.
Now I'm ready for breakfast.

Thank you, Daddy, for helping me put on my nice, warm coat.
I can button two buttons.
Thank you for wrapping my red scarf around my neck,
    and for snapping my cap under my chin, where it tickles.
Thank you for putting my mittens on my hands.
Now they won't get cold.

Thank you, God, for the church house and for my teacher.
Thank you 'cause Mommy and Daddy take me to church with them.
Thank you for Mommy and Daddy.

© MCMLXIII, The Standard Publishing Company

God Gave Me Berries

Good, red strawberries!
Daddy and I picked them from a bush.
Daddy showed me the ones that were ripe,
   and I pulled them by the green part
   and put them in a basket.

Mommy washed the strawberries in cold water.
I like to hold them by the stem and bite the red part.
Berries are sweet, and juice runs down my chin;
And sometimes it gets on my hands.

I throw the green parts of the berries away,
   but I eat all the red parts.
Then I wash my hands.
My mouth still tastes like berries,
   and my tongue is very red.

Thank you, God, for berries.

© MCMLXIII, The Standard Publishing Company

God Gave Me Food

One time when Jesus was teaching a crowd of people, He said, "Look at the birds that fly in the air. They do not plant food and put it into barns, but your heavenly Father feeds them. And you are worth more than birds.

"Do not worry about whether you will have something to eat and something to drink. Your heavenly Father knows everything you need."

From Matthew 6:25, 26, 31, 32

Heavenly Father,
Thank you for food
That my mother fixes
(It tastes very good):
A tall glass of milk,
Cold and white,
My bowl full of cereal
(I eat every bite),
Meat and vegetables,
Soft mashed potatoes,
Butter and bread,
Sweet, red tomatoes,
And cake and ice cream
(A very nice treat);
Thank you for everything
I like to eat. Amen.

MCMLXIII, The Standard Publishing Company

God Gave Me Clothes

My daddy gave me a new coat for my birthday.
I'm a year older now.
My coat is brown and soft like my teddy bear.

"Now put this arm in," Daddy said.
"Now this one."
The coat felt funny. It was crooked.
But Daddy fixed it. He buttoned each button—
    one, two, three, four, five buttons.

Then Daddy and I looked in the big mirror.
I liked my new coat.
I laughed, and Daddy laughed too.
Then he gave me a big hug around the middle.

"Thank you, Daddy, for my coat."

MCMLXIII, The Standard Publishing Company

God Gave Me Toys

I like to play with my toys.
I like to play house.
I sit in my rocking chair
   and rock my baby doll to sleep.
Then I put her in bed and sing a little song to her
   like the one Mommy sings to me.

Sometimes I like to play zoo.
I pretend each one of my animals is in a cage.
Then baby doll and I go to the zoo
   and look at each animal.

I say, "Grrr!" for my kitty
   and pretend she is a big lion.
And baby doll and I hurry past the elephant's cage
   so he won't squirt water on us
   with his big, gray trunk.

Pretending is lots of fun,
   but do you know what I like to do best of all?
I like to play with my friends,
   Bobby, and Susan, and Rachel.
Toys are more fun when we all play together.

MCMLXIII, The Standard Publishing Company

God Gave Me Flowers

One day Mommy and I planted little brown things called bulbs. We planted them in the soft dirt by our house. Mommy said, "After a while we will have pretty flowers in our yard."

Every day I looked outside at the ground. And every day all I saw was dark brown dirt. Sometimes the rain came down and made mud. Then the sun shone and dried the mud and made it dirt again.

"When will we have pretty flowers in our yard, Mommy?"

"In a few more days," she said. "Flowers need plenty of water and sunshine before they are ready to grow."

One day I saw something green sticking up out of the ground. "Is that a flower?" I asked Mommy. "No, it is a leaf. Soon we will have flowers."

Every day I looked. Every day the leaf was taller. Every day Mommy said, "Our flowers will grow."

After breakfast one day, Mommy said, "Look in the yard today. Look where we planted the bulbs."

I did look. Do you know what I saw? Flowers! Yellow flowers were on the ends of the tall, green leaves.

"They are pretty," I said.

"Yes," said Mommy. "God made the pretty yellow flowers to grow for you."

Hook

CMLXIII, The Standard Publishing Company

God Gave Me Rain

"Plop—zip! Plop—zip!" The rain makes a funny sound on my umbrella. Each drop goes "plop," then it rolls down my silky umbrella, "zip." From underneath it looks like a lot of tiny rivers running down the top of my umbrella.

Raindrops run right off my raincoat. It's slippery, and they slide right off. Sometimes little drops of water stay on the back of my hands. And they are hard to shake off.

"Splash! Splash!" go my boots when I walk in a little puddle. If I splash too hard, water gets inside my boots. Wet socks don't feel good, and Mommy doesn't like them either.

Sometimes I move the toe of one boot back and forth slowly in the water. "Swish. Swish."

Rain is pretty. It's red on my umbrella, on my raincoat, and on my boots. It's green on the grass, and gray on the sidewalk. It's all different colors in the puddles. And after it stops raining, little drops of water on grass and leaves shine like diamonds.

Rain makes everything outside smell good.

Thank you, God, for the rain.

MCMLXIII, The Standard Publishing Company

God Gave Me Bible School

I like to go to Bible school. My kind teacher smiles and says, "Come in. You look very pretty today." Then I put my money in the basket. That is one way we say, "I love you, God."

I like to go to Bible school. Every Sunday I get to see Paula and Billy and Freddie and Roger. But sometimes one of us is sick.

Sometimes we look at pictures on the table. The one I like best is a picture of Jesus.

We sing and pray and listen to Teacher tell us a story from God's Book. One time he told us that Jesus put mud on a blind man's eyes and made him see again. We looked at a picture of Jesus and the blind man.

Teacher said, "Aren't you glad God gave us Jesus?"

"Yes," we said. Then we closed our eyes and prayed, "Thank you, God, for Jesus."

And I said in my head where no one else can hear, "Thank you, God, for my teacher and for Bible school. Amen."

MCMLXIII, The Standard Publishing Company

God Gave Me My Dog

I have a little puppy named Sandy. I show Sandy I love him by patting his head and rubbing his neck. His hair feels soft and smooth. Sandy likes for me to pat him.

I take good care of Sandy. I give him good dog food and plenty of water. I play with him and fix his bed for him. Sandy likes that.

When I take care of Sandy, he licks my face and wags his tail.

When someone does something for me, I say "Thank you.

Licking my face and wagging his tail is how Sandy says "Thank you."

Thank you, God, for my dog Sandy.

© MCMLXIII The Standard Publishing Company

God Gave Me Birds

One day my mother said, "Come and look out the window, but be very quiet." So I walked on my tiptoes over to the window with Mommy. She put a finger over her mouth. "Shhh," she said. And she pointed outside to the tree in our back yard.

There on a big, black branch was a little round dish made out of dry grass. Mommy whispered, "That's a bird's nest. Look at the mother bird feeding her babies."

The little baby birds must have been very hungry because they opened their mouths very wide and made a lot of noise. "Chirp! Chirp!" And the mother bird gave each baby bird a worm to eat.

Mommy said, "God makes sure that every bird has food to eat."

And God gives me food too.

Thank you, God, for taking care of the birds and for taking care of me.

© MCMLXIII, The Standard Publishing Company

God Gave Me Squirrels

A friendly, fuzzy little squirrel
Lives high up in a tree.
I watch him from my window,
But he never looks at me.

When summertime is nearly gone,
And leaves begin to fall,
My squirrel friend takes nuts to his tree—
He holds them in his jaw.

He holds them carefully in a hole
Where only squirrels can go;
He has to hide them now, before
The ground is white with snow.

So all year long the squirrel has food
For all his family.
God takes care of friendly squirrels
And children just like me.

CMLXIII, The Standard Publishing Company

God Gave Me Day

Thank you, God, for mornings
   when I can wake up and wash my face
   and put clean clothes on, all by myself.

Thank you for mornings
   when Mommy gives me a big hug and kiss
   and says, "Good morning, dear.
   What would you like for breakfast?"

And thank you for the fun I have
   playing with my doll and with my friends
   outside in the daytime.

Thank you for the pretty blue sky,
   and the yellow sunshine, and the flowers
   that smell so good,
   and for the bees that hum, "Bzzzz. Bzzzz."

Thank you for afternoons
   when Daddy comes home.

Thank you, God, for every thing
   that makes me happy all day long.

CMLXIII, The Standard Publishing Company

God Gave Me Night

When I look out the window at night, the sky is dark, dark blue and the sun is all gone. That's so we can sleep. I see a big, white, shiny moon that looks like a big, smiling face.

Sometimes the moonlight shines right in the window. I can see it on the floor, and when I put my hand down to touch it, the moonlight shines on me.

Everywhere I look in the sky, there are little white stars that sparkle.

Sometimes I put my eyes right next to the window and look just as far as I can into the sky. And I know that God is up there 'way past the stars, the moon, and everything.

God is up there where no one can see Him, but where He can see everyone.

And He's taking care of people 'way down here.

LXIII, The Standard Publishing Company

God Gave Me Bed

When night comes and it's dark outside, and I'm sleepy and start to yawn, my mother helps me get ready for bed.

I take a bath and splash a little and have fun. Mommy dries me with a big towel that almost covers me up. I climb into my soft, warm pajamas. They feel so-o-o good!

After I run and kiss Daddy good night, I get down on my knees beside my bed and talk to God. I say "Thank you" to God for Mommy and Daddy and all the good times I've had that day.

Mommy pulls back the covers on my bed, and I hurry and climb in with my teddy bear. Then Mommy covers me up to my neck and tucks some covers under my feet. Mommy kisses me good night, and I hug her and kiss her real big. Then Mommy turns out the light.

That's when teddy and I go to sleep until the morning.

Thank you, God, for my nice soft bed and pillow.

MLXIII, The Standard Publishing Company